THIS B
BELONGS TO

_____

_____

_____

Wolf Mountain Press

RV Maintenance Log

CHASSIS

Date _____

Year _____ Make _____ Model _____ Serial # _____

Check	Condition	Check	Condition
Tire Pressure		Battery/Alternator	
Tire Wear/Age		Vehicle Lights	
Wheel Rims		Windshield Wipers	
Wheel Bearing/Seal		Tow Hitch	
Brake System		Switches	
Engine Oil		Mirrors	
Transmission		Differential	
Filters		Wiring	
Heating System		Belts and Hoses	
Cooling System		Power Steering	
Suspension/Shocks		Fuel Filter	
Water Pump		Chassis Lube	
Frame/Fastners		Cruise Control	
Air Conditioner		Horn	
Exhaust System		Airbags	
Gas Tank & Cap		Seatbelts	

Miles _____

Engine Oil Type _____

Notes _____

RV Maintenance Log
COACH BODY

Date _____

Year _____ Make _____ Model _____ Serial # _____

Check	Condition	Check	Condition
Dump Valve		Interior Lights	
Grey Water Tank		Air Conditioner	
Black Water Tank		Window Seals	
Fresh Water Tank		Window Locks	
Water Pump		Door Locks	
Converter Ele. Sys.		Roof Vents	
Generator		Fire Extinguisher	
Refrigererator		First Aid Kit	
Stove		Power Steps	
Microwave		Awnings	
Furnace		Slide Seals	
Coach Battery		Exterior Storage	
Water Heater		Smoke Detector	
Shower & Sinks		CO Detector	
Toilet		Upholstery	
Storage Cabinets		Roof Membrane	

Miles _____   Generator Engine Oil Type _____

Notes _____

RV Maintenance Log

CHASSIS

Date _____

Year _____ Make _____ Model _____ Serial # _____

Check	Condition	Check	Condition
Tire Pressure		Battery/Alternator	
Tire Wear/Age		Vehicle Lights	
Wheel Rims		Windshield Wipers	
Wheel Bearing/Seal		Tow Hitch	
Brake System		Switches	
Engine Oil		Mirrors	
Transmission		Differential	
Filters		Wiring	
Heating System		Belts and Hoses	
Cooling System		Power Steering	
Suspension/Shocks		Fuel Filter	
Water Pump		Chassis Lube	
Frame/Fastners		Cruise Control	
Air Conditioner		Horn	
Exhaust System		Airbags	
Gas Tank & Cap		Seatbelts	

Miles _____   Engine Oil Type _____

Notes _____

RV Maintenance Log

COACH BODY

Date _____

Year _____ Make _____ Model _____ Serial # _____

Check	Condition	Check	Condition
Dump Valve		Interior Lights	
Grey Water Tank		Air Conditioner	
Black Water Tank		Window Seals	
Fresh Water Tank		Window Locks	
Water Pump		Door Locks	
Converter Ele. Sys.		Roof Vents	
Generator		Fire Extinguisher	
Refrigererator		First Aid Kit	
Stove		Power Steps	
Microwave		Awnings	
Furnace		Slide Seals	
Coach Battery		Exterior Storage	
Water Heater		Smoke Detector	
Shower & Sinks		CO Detector	
Toilet		Upholstery	
Storage Cabinets		Roof Membrane	

Miles _____   Generator Engine Oil Type _____

Notes _____

RV Maintenance Log
CHASSIS

Date _____

Year _____ Make _____ Model _____ Serial # _____

Check	Condition	Check	Condition
Tire Pressure		Battery/Alternator	
Tire Wear/Age		Vehicle Lights	
Wheel Rims		Windshield Wipers	
Wheel Bearing/Seal		Tow Hitch	
Brake System		Switches	
Engine Oil		Mirrors	
Transmission		Differential	
Filters		Wiring	
Heating System		Belts and Hoses	
Cooling System		Power Steering	
Suspension/Shocks		Fuel Filter	
Water Pump		Chassis Lube	
Frame/Fastners		Cruise Control	
Air Conditioner		Horn	
Exhaust System		Airbags	
Gas Tank & Cap		Seatbelts	

Miles _____

Engine Oil Type _____

Notes _____

RV Maintenance Log

COACH BODY

Date _____

Year _____ Make _____ Model _____ Serial # _____

Check	Condition	Check	Condition
Dump Valve		Interior Lights	
Grey Water Tank		Air Conditioner	
Black Water Tank		Window Seals	
Fresh Water Tank		Window Locks	
Water Pump		Door Locks	
Converter Ele. Sys.		Roof Vents	
Generator		Fire Extinguisher	
Refrigererator		First Aid Kit	
Stove		Power Steps	
Microwave		Awnings	
Furnace		Slide Seals	
Coach Battery		Exterior Storage	
Water Heater		Smoke Detector	
Shower & Sinks		CO Detector	
Toilet		Upholstery	
Storage Cabinets		Roof Membrane	

Miles _____   Generator Engine Oil Type _____

Notes _____

RV Maintenance Log
CHASSIS

Date _____

Year _____ Make _____ Model _____ Serial # _____

Check	Condition	Check	Condition
Tire Pressure		Battery/Alternator	
Tire Wear/Age		Vehicle Lights	
Wheel Rims		Windshield Wipers	
Wheel Bearing/Seal		Tow Hitch	
Brake System		Switches	
Engine Oil		Mirrors	
Transmission		Differential	
Filters		Wiring	
Heating System		Belts and Hoses	
Cooling System		Power Steering	
Suspension/Shocks		Fuel Filter	
Water Pump		Chassis Lube	
Frame/Fastners		Cruise Control	
Air Conditioner		Horn	
Exhaust System		Airbags	
Gas Tank & Cap		Seatbelts	

Miles _____   Engine Oil Type _____

Notes _____

RV Maintenance Log

COACH BODY

Date _____

Year _____ Make _____ Model _____ Serial # _____

Check	Condition	Check	Condition
Dump Valve		Interior Lights	
Grey Water Tank		Air Conditioner	
Black Water Tank		Window Seals	
Fresh Water Tank		Window Locks	
Water Pump		Door Locks	
Converter Ele. Sys.		Roof Vents	
Generator		Fire Extinguisher	
Refrigererator		First Aid Kit	
Stove		Power Steps	
Microwave		Awnings	
Furnace		Slide Seals	
Coach Battery		Exterior Storage	
Water Heater		Smoke Detector	
Shower & Sinks		CO Detector	
Toilet		Upholstery	
Storage Cabinets		Roof Membrane	

Miles _____   Generator Engine Oil Type _____

Notes _____

RV Maintenance Log

CHASSIS

Date _____

Year _____ Make _____ Model _____ Serial # _____

Check	Condition	Check	Condition
Tire Pressure		Battery/Alternator	
Tire Wear/Age		Vehicle Lights	
Wheel Rims		Windshield Wipers	
Wheel Bearing/Seal		Tow Hitch	
Brake System		Switches	
Engine Oil		Mirrors	
Transmission		Differential	
Filters		Wiring	
Heating System		Belts and Hoses	
Cooling System		Power Steering	
Suspension/Shocks		Fuel Filter	
Water Pump		Chassis Lube	
Frame/Fastners		Cruise Control	
Air Conditioner		Horn	
Exhaust System		Airbags	
Gas Tank & Cap		Seatbelts	

Miles _____   Engine Oil Type _____

Notes _____

RV Maintenance Log
COACH BODY

Date _____

Year _____ Make _____ Model _____ Serial # _____

Check	Condition	Check	Condition
Dump Valve		Interior Lights	
Grey Water Tank		Air Conditioner	
Black Water Tank		Window Seals	
Fresh Water Tank		Window Locks	
Water Pump		Door Locks	
Converter Ele. Sys.		Roof Vents	
Generator		Fire Extinguisher	
Refrigererator		First Aid Kit	
Stove		Power Steps	
Microwave		Awnings	
Furnace		Slide Seals	
Coach Battery		Exterior Storage	
Water Heater		Smoke Detector	
Shower & Sinks		CO Detector	
Toilet		Upholstery	
Storage Cabinets		Roof Membrane	

Miles _____   Generator Engine Oil Type _____

Notes _____

RV Maintenance Log

CHASSIS

RECREATIONAL VEHICLE
★ MAINTENANCE ★
— LOG —

Date _____

Year _____ Make _____ Model _____ Serial # _____

Check	Condition	Check	Condition
Tire Pressure		Battery/Alternator	
Tire Wear/Age		Vehicle Lights	
Wheel Rims		Windshield Wipers	
Wheel Bearing/Seal		Tow Hitch	
Brake System		Switches	
Engine Oil		Mirrors	
Transmission		Differential	
Filters		Wiring	
Heating System		Belts and Hoses	
Cooling System		Power Steering	
Suspension/Shocks		Fuel Filter	
Water Pump		Chassis Lube	
Frame/Fastners		Cruise Control	
Air Conditioner		Horn	
Exhaust System		Airbags	
Gas Tank & Cap		Seatbelts	

Miles _____   Engine Oil Type _____

Notes _____

RV Maintenance Log

COACH BODY

Date _____

Year _____ Make _____ Model _____ Serial # _____

Check	Condition	Check	Condition
Dump Valve		Interior Lights	
Grey Water Tank		Air Conditioner	
Black Water Tank		Window Seals	
Fresh Water Tank		Window Locks	
Water Pump		Door Locks	
Converter Ele. Sys.		Roof Vents	
Generator		Fire Extinguisher	
Refrigererator		First Aid Kit	
Stove		Power Steps	
Microwave		Awnings	
Furnace		Slide Seals	
Coach Battery		Exterior Storage	
Water Heater		Smoke Detector	
Shower & Sinks		CO Detector	
Toilet		Upholstery	
Storage Cabinets		Roof Membrane	

Miles _____   Generator Engine Oil Type _____

Notes _____

RV Maintenance Log
CHASSIS

Date _____

Year _____ Make _____ Model _____ Serial # _____

Check	Condition	Check	Condition
Tire Pressure		Battery/Alternator	
Tire Wear/Age		Vehicle Lights	
Wheel Rims		Windshield Wipers	
Wheel Bearing/Seal		Tow Hitch	
Brake System		Switches	
Engine Oil		Mirrors	
Transmission		Differential	
Filters		Wiring	
Heating System		Belts and Hoses	
Cooling System		Power Steering	
Suspension/Shocks		Fuel Filter	
Water Pump		Chassis Lube	
Frame/Fastners		Cruise Control	
Air Conditioner		Horn	
Exhaust System		Airbags	
Gas Tank & Cap		Seatbelts	

Miles _____

Engine Oil Type _____

Notes _____

RV Maintenance Log
COACH BODY

RECREATIONAL VEHICLE
★ MAINTENANCE ★
LOG

Date

Year _____   Make _____   Model _____   Serial # _____

Check	Condition	Check	Condition
Dump Valve		Interior Lights	
Grey Water Tank		Air Conditioner	
Black Water Tank		Window Seals	
Fresh Water Tank		Window Locks	
Water Pump		Door Locks	
Converter Ele. Sys.		Roof Vents	
Generator		Fire Extinguisher	
Refrigererator		First Aid Kit	
Stove		Power Steps	
Microwave		Awnings	
Furnace		Slide Seals	
Coach Battery		Exterior Storage	
Water Heater		Smoke Detector	
Shower & Sinks		CO Detector	
Toilet		Upholstery	
Storage Cabinets		Roof Membrane	

Miles _____   Generator Engine Oil Type _____

Notes _____

RV Maintenance Log

CHASSIS

Date _____

Year _____ Make _____ Model _____ Serial # _____

Check	Condition	Check	Condition
Tire Pressure		Battery/Alternator	
Tire Wear/Age		Vehicle Lights	
Wheel Rims		Windshield Wipers	
Wheel Bearing/Seal		Tow Hitch	
Brake System		Switches	
Engine Oil		Mirrors	
Transmission		Differential	
Filters		Wiring	
Heating System		Belts and Hoses	
Cooling System		Power Steering	
Suspension/Shocks		Fuel Filter	
Water Pump		Chassis Lube	
Frame/Fastners		Cruise Control	
Air Conditioner		Horn	
Exhaust System		Airbags	
Gas Tank & Cap		Seatbelts	

Miles _____

Engine Oil Type _____

Notes _____

RV Maintenance Log
COACH BODY

Date _____

Year _____ Make _____ Model _____ Serial # _____

Check	Condition	Check	Condition
Dump Valve		Interior Lights	
Grey Water Tank		Air Conditioner	
Black Water Tank		Window Seals	
Fresh Water Tank		Window Locks	
Water Pump		Door Locks	
Converter Ele. Sys.		Roof Vents	
Generator		Fire Extinguisher	
Refrigererator		First Aid Kit	
Stove		Power Steps	
Microwave		Awnings	
Furnace		Slide Seals	
Coach Battery		Exterior Storage	
Water Heater		Smoke Detector	
Shower & Sinks		CO Detector	
Toilet		Upholstery	
Storage Cabinets		Roof Membrane	

Miles _____   Generator Engine Oil Type _____

Notes _____

RV Maintenance Log

CHASSIS

Date _____

Year _____ Make _____ Model _____ Serial # _____

Check	Condition	Check	Condition
Tire Pressure		Battery/Alternator	
Tire Wear/Age		Vehicle Lights	
Wheel Rims		Windshield Wipers	
Wheel Bearing/Seal		Tow Hitch	
Brake System		Switches	
Engine Oil		Mirrors	
Transmission		Differential	
Filters		Wiring	
Heating System		Belts and Hoses	
Cooling System		Power Steering	
Suspension/Shocks		Fuel Filter	
Water Pump		Chassis Lube	
Frame/Fastners		Cruise Control	
Air Conditioner		Horn	
Exhaust System		Airbags	
Gas Tank & Cap		Seatbelts	

Miles _____   Engine Oil Type _____

Notes _____

RV Maintenance Log

COACH BODY

Date _____

Year _____ Make _____ Model _____ Serial # _____

Check	Condition	Check	Condition
Dump Valve		Interior Lights	
Grey Water Tank		Air Conditioner	
Black Water Tank		Window Seals	
Fresh Water Tank		Window Locks	
Water Pump		Door Locks	
Converter Ele. Sys.		Roof Vents	
Generator		Fire Extinguisher	
Refrigererator		First Aid Kit	
Stove		Power Steps	
Microwave		Awnings	
Furnace		Slide Seals	
Coach Battery		Exterior Storage	
Water Heater		Smoke Detector	
Shower & Sinks		CO Detector	
Toilet		Upholstery	
Storage Cabinets		Roof Membrane	

Miles _____   Generator Engine Oil Type _____

Notes _____

RV Maintenance Log
CHASSIS

Date _____

Year _____ Make _____ Model _____ Serial # _____

Check	Condition	Check	Condition
Tire Pressure		Battery/Alternator	
Tire Wear/Age		Vehicle Lights	
Wheel Rims		Windshield Wipers	
Wheel Bearing/Seal		Tow Hitch	
Brake System		Switches	
Engine Oil		Mirrors	
Transmission		Differential	
Filters		Wiring	
Heating System		Belts and Hoses	
Cooling System		Power Steering	
Suspension/Shocks		Fuel Filter	
Water Pump		Chassis Lube	
Frame/Fastners		Cruise Control	
Air Conditioner		Horn	
Exhaust System		Airbags	
Gas Tank & Cap		Seatbelts	

Miles _____   Engine Oil Type _____

Notes _____

RV Maintenance Log

COACH BODY

Date _____

Year _____ Make _____ Model _____ Serial # _____

Check	Condition	Check	Condition
Dump Valve		Interior Lights	
Grey Water Tank		Air Conditioner	
Black Water Tank		Window Seals	
Fresh Water Tank		Window Locks	
Water Pump		Door Locks	
Converter Ele. Sys.		Roof Vents	
Generator		Fire Extinguisher	
Refrigererator		First Aid Kit	
Stove		Power Steps	
Microwave		Awnings	
Furnace		Slide Seals	
Coach Battery		Exterior Storage	
Water Heater		Smoke Detector	
Shower & Sinks		CO Detector	
Toilet		Upholstery	
Storage Cabinets		Roof Membrane	

Miles _____ Generator Engine Oil Type _____

Notes _____

RV Maintenance Log

CHASSIS

Date _____

Year _____ Make _____ Model _____ Serial # _____

Check	Condition	Check	Condition
Tire Pressure		Battery/Alternator	
Tire Wear/Age		Vehicle Lights	
Wheel Rims		Windshield Wipers	
Wheel Bearing/Seal		Tow Hitch	
Brake System		Switches	
Engine Oil		Mirrors	
Transmission		Differential	
Filters		Wiring	
Heating System		Belts and Hoses	
Cooling System		Power Steering	
Suspension/Shocks		Fuel Filter	
Water Pump		Chassis Lube	
Frame/Fastners		Cruise Control	
Air Conditioner		Horn	
Exhaust System		Airbags	
Gas Tank & Cap		Seatbelts	

Miles _____   Engine Oil Type _____

Notes _____

RV Maintenance Log

CHASSIS

Date _____

Year _____ Make _____ Model _____ Serial # _____

Check	Condition	Check	Condition
Tire Pressure		Battery/Alternator	
Tire Wear/Age		Vehicle Lights	
Wheel Rims		Windshield Wipers	
Wheel Bearing/Seal		Tow Hitch	
Brake System		Switches	
Engine Oil		Mirrors	
Transmission		Differential	
Filters		Wiring	
Heating System		Belts and Hoses	
Cooling System		Power Steering	
Suspension/Shocks		Fuel Filter	
Water Pump		Chassis Lube	
Frame/Fastners		Cruise Control	
Air Conditioner		Horn	
Exhaust System		Airbags	
Gas Tank & Cap		Seatbelts	

Miles _____   Engine Oil Type _____

Notes _____

RV Maintenance Log

CHASSIS

Date _____

Year _____ Make _____ Model _____ Serial # _____

Check	Condition	Check	Condition
Tire Pressure		Battery/Alternator	
Tire Wear/Age		Vehicle Lights	
Wheel Rims		Windshield Wipers	
Wheel Bearing/Seal		Tow Hitch	
Brake System		Switches	
Engine Oil		Mirrors	
Transmission		Differential	
Filters		Wiring	
Heating System		Belts and Hoses	
Cooling System		Power Steering	
Suspension/Shocks		Fuel Filter	
Water Pump		Chassis Lube	
Frame/Fastners		Cruise Control	
Air Conditioner		Horn	
Exhaust System		Airbags	
Gas Tank & Cap		Seatbelts	

Miles _____   Engine Oil Type _____

Notes _____

RV Maintenance Log

COACH BODY

Date _____

Year _____ Make _____ Model _____ Serial # _____

Check	Condition	Check	Condition
Dump Valve		Interior Lights	
Grey Water Tank		Air Conditioner	
Black Water Tank		Window Seals	
Fresh Water Tank		Window Locks	
Water Pump		Door Locks	
Converter Ele. Sys.		Roof Vents	
Generator		Fire Extinguisher	
Refrigererator		First Aid Kit	
Stove		Power Steps	
Microwave		Awnings	
Furnace		Slide Seals	
Coach Battery		Exterior Storage	
Water Heater		Smoke Detector	
Shower & Sinks		CO Detector	
Toilet		Upholstery	
Storage Cabinets		Roof Membrane	

Miles _____   Generator Engine Oil Type _____

Notes _____

RV Maintenance Log
CHASSIS

Date _____

Year _____ Make _____ Model _____ Serial # _____

Check	Condition	Check	Condition
Tire Pressure		Battery/Alternator	
Tire Wear/Age		Vehicle Lights	
Wheel Rims		Windshield Wipers	
Wheel Bearing/Seal		Tow Hitch	
Brake System		Switches	
Engine Oil		Mirrors	
Transmission		Differential	
Filters		Wiring	
Heating System		Belts and Hoses	
Cooling System		Power Steering	
Suspension/Shocks		Fuel Filter	
Water Pump		Chassis Lube	
Frame/Fastners		Cruise Control	
Air Conditioner		Horn	
Exhaust System		Airbags	
Gas Tank & Cap		Seatbelts	

Miles _____   Engine Oil Type _____

Notes _____

RV Maintenance Log

COACH BODY

RECREATIONAL VEHICLE — MAINTENANCE LOG

Date _____

Year _____ Make _____ Model _____ Serial # _____

Check	Condition	Check	Condition
Dump Valve		Interior Lights	
Grey Water Tank		Air Conditioner	
Black Water Tank		Window Seals	
Fresh Water Tank		Window Locks	
Water Pump		Door Locks	
Converter Ele. Sys.		Roof Vents	
Generator		Fire Extinguisher	
Refrigererator		First Aid Kit	
Stove		Power Steps	
Microwave		Awnings	
Furnace		Slide Seals	
Coach Battery		Exterior Storage	
Water Heater		Smoke Detector	
Shower & Sinks		CO Detector	
Toilet		Upholstery	
Storage Cabinets		Roof Membrane	

Miles _____

Generator Engine Oil Type _____

Notes _____

RV Maintenance Log

CHASSIS

Date _____

Year _____ Make _____ Model _____ Serial # _____

Check	Condition	Check	Condition
Tire Pressure		Battery/Alternator	
Tire Wear/Age		Vehicle Lights	
Wheel Rims		Windshield Wipers	
Wheel Bearing/Seal		Tow Hitch	
Brake System		Switches	
Engine Oil		Mirrors	
Transmission		Differential	
Filters		Wiring	
Heating System		Belts and Hoses	
Cooling System		Power Steering	
Suspension/Shocks		Fuel Filter	
Water Pump		Chassis Lube	
Frame/Fastners		Cruise Control	
Air Conditioner		Horn	
Exhaust System		Airbags	
Gas Tank & Cap		Seatbelts	

Miles _____   Engine Oil Type _____

Notes _____

RV Maintenance Log

COACH BODY

Date _____

Year _____ Make _____ Model _____ Serial # _____

Check	Condition	Check	Condition
Dump Valve		Interior Lights	
Grey Water Tank		Air Conditioner	
Black Water Tank		Window Seals	
Fresh Water Tank		Window Locks	
Water Pump		Door Locks	
Converter Ele. Sys.		Roof Vents	
Generator		Fire Extinguisher	
Refrigererator		First Aid Kit	
Stove		Power Steps	
Microwave		Awnings	
Furnace		Slide Seals	
Coach Battery		Exterior Storage	
Water Heater		Smoke Detector	
Shower & Sinks		CO Detector	
Toilet		Upholstery	
Storage Cabinets		Roof Membrane	

Miles _____   Generator Engine Oil Type _____

Notes _____

RV Maintenance Log

CHASSIS

Date _____

Year _____ Make _____ Model _____ Serial # _____

Check	Condition	Check	Condition
Tire Pressure		Battery/Alternator	
Tire Wear/Age		Vehicle Lights	
Wheel Rims		Windshield Wipers	
Wheel Bearing/Seal		Tow Hitch	
Brake System		Switches	
Engine Oil		Mirrors	
Transmission		Differential	
Filters		Wiring	
Heating System		Belts and Hoses	
Cooling System		Power Steering	
Suspension/Shocks		Fuel Filter	
Water Pump		Chassis Lube	
Frame/Fastners		Cruise Control	
Air Conditioner		Horn	
Exhaust System		Airbags	
Gas Tank & Cap		Seatbelts	

Miles _____   Engine Oil Type _____

Notes _____

RV Maintenance Log

COACH BODY

RECREATIONAL VEHICLE
★ MAINTENANCE ★
— LOG —

Date _____

Year _____ Make _____ Model _____ Serial # _____

Check	Condition	Check	Condition
Dump Valve		Interior Lights	
Grey Water Tank		Air Conditioner	
Black Water Tank		Window Seals	
Fresh Water Tank		Window Locks	
Water Pump		Door Locks	
Converter Ele. Sys.		Roof Vents	
Generator		Fire Extinguisher	
Refrigererator		First Aid Kit	
Stove		Power Steps	
Microwave		Awnings	
Furnace		Slide Seals	
Coach Battery		Exterior Storage	
Water Heater		Smoke Detector	
Shower & Sinks		CO Detector	
Toilet		Upholstery	
Storage Cabinets		Roof Membrane	

Miles _____   Generator Engine Oil Type _____

Notes _____

RV Maintenance Log
CHASSIS

Date _____

Year _____ Make _____ Model _____ Serial # _____

Check	Condition	Check	Condition
Tire Pressure		Battery/Alternator	
Tire Wear/Age		Vehicle Lights	
Wheel Rims		Windshield Wipers	
Wheel Bearing/Seal		Tow Hitch	
Brake System		Switches	
Engine Oil		Mirrors	
Transmission		Differential	
Filters		Wiring	
Heating System		Belts and Hoses	
Cooling System		Power Steering	
Suspension/Shocks		Fuel Filter	
Water Pump		Chassis Lube	
Frame/Fastners		Cruise Control	
Air Conditioner		Horn	
Exhaust System		Airbags	
Gas Tank & Cap		Seatbelts	

Miles _____   Engine Oil Type _____

Notes _____

RV Maintenance Log

COACH BODY

RECREATIONAL VEHICLE
★ MAINTENANCE ★
— LOG —

Date _____

Year _____   Make _____   Model _____   Serial # _____

Check	Condition	Check	Condition
Dump Valve		Interior Lights	
Grey Water Tank		Air Conditioner	
Black Water Tank		Window Seals	
Fresh Water Tank		Window Locks	
Water Pump		Door Locks	
Converter Ele. Sys.		Roof Vents	
Generator		Fire Extinguisher	
Refrigererator		First Aid Kit	
Stove		Power Steps	
Microwave		Awnings	
Furnace		Slide Seals	
Coach Battery		Exterior Storage	
Water Heater		Smoke Detector	
Shower & Sinks		CO Detector	
Toilet		Upholstery	
Storage Cabinets		Roof Membrane	

Miles _____   Generator Engine Oil Type _____

Notes _____

RV Maintenance Log

CHASSIS

Date _____

Year _____ Make _____ Model _____ Serial # _____

Check	Condition	Check	Condition
Tire Pressure		Battery/Alternator	
Tire Wear/Age		Vehicle Lights	
Wheel Rims		Windshield Wipers	
Wheel Bearing/Seal		Tow Hitch	
Brake System		Switches	
Engine Oil		Mirrors	
Transmission		Differential	
Filters		Wiring	
Heating System		Belts and Hoses	
Cooling System		Power Steering	
Suspension/Shocks		Fuel Filter	
Water Pump		Chassis Lube	
Frame/Fastners		Cruise Control	
Air Conditioner		Horn	
Exhaust System		Airbags	
Gas Tank & Cap		Seatbelts	

Miles _____   Engine Oil Type _____

Notes _____

RV Maintenance Log

COACH BODY

Date _____

Year _____ Make _____ Model _____ Serial # _____

Check	Condition	Check	Condition
Dump Valve		Interior Lights	
Grey Water Tank		Air Conditioner	
Black Water Tank		Window Seals	
Fresh Water Tank		Window Locks	
Water Pump		Door Locks	
Converter Ele. Sys.		Roof Vents	
Generator		Fire Extinguisher	
Refrigererator		First Aid Kit	
Stove		Power Steps	
Microwave		Awnings	
Furnace		Slide Seals	
Coach Battery		Exterior Storage	
Water Heater		Smoke Detector	
Shower & Sinks		CO Detector	
Toilet		Upholstery	
Storage Cabinets		Roof Membrane	

Miles _____

Generator Engine Oil Type _____

Notes _____

RV Maintenance Log

CHASSIS

Date _____

Year _____ Make _____ Model _____ Serial # _____

Check	Condition	Check	Condition
Tire Pressure		Battery/Alternator	
Tire Wear/Age		Vehicle Lights	
Wheel Rims		Windshield Wipers	
Wheel Bearing/Seal		Tow Hitch	
Brake System		Switches	
Engine Oil		Mirrors	
Transmission		Differential	
Filters		Wiring	
Heating System		Belts and Hoses	
Cooling System		Power Steering	
Suspension/Shocks		Fuel Filter	
Water Pump		Chassis Lube	
Frame/Fastners		Cruise Control	
Air Conditioner		Horn	
Exhaust System		Airbags	
Gas Tank & Cap		Seatbelts	

Miles _____   Engine Oil Type _____

Notes _____

RV Maintenance Log
COACH BODY

Date _____

Year _____ Make _____ Model _____ Serial # _____

Check	Condition	Check	Condition
Dump Valve		Interior Lights	
Grey Water Tank		Air Conditioner	
Black Water Tank		Window Seals	
Fresh Water Tank		Window Locks	
Water Pump		Door Locks	
Converter Ele. Sys.		Roof Vents	
Generator		Fire Extinguisher	
Refrigererator		First Aid Kit	
Stove		Power Steps	
Microwave		Awnings	
Furnace		Slide Seals	
Coach Battery		Exterior Storage	
Water Heater		Smoke Detector	
Shower & Sinks		CO Detector	
Toilet		Upholstery	
Storage Cabinets		Roof Membrane	

Miles _____   Generator Engine Oil Type _____

Notes _____

RV Maintenance Log

CHASSIS

Date _____

Year _____ Make _____ Model _____ Serial # _____

Check	Condition	Check	Condition
Tire Pressure		Battery/Alternator	
Tire Wear/Age		Vehicle Lights	
Wheel Rims		Windshield Wipers	
Wheel Bearing/Seal		Tow Hitch	
Brake System		Switches	
Engine Oil		Mirrors	
Transmission		Differential	
Filters		Wiring	
Heating System		Belts and Hoses	
Cooling System		Power Steering	
Suspension/Shocks		Fuel Filter	
Water Pump		Chassis Lube	
Frame/Fastners		Cruise Control	
Air Conditioner		Horn	
Exhaust System		Airbags	
Gas Tank & Cap		Seatbelts	

Miles _____   Engine Oil Type _____

Notes _____

RV Maintenance Log
COACH BODY

Date _____

Year _____ Make _____ Model _____ Serial # _____

Check	Condition	Check	Condition
Dump Valve		Interior Lights	
Grey Water Tank		Air Conditioner	
Black Water Tank		Window Seals	
Fresh Water Tank		Window Locks	
Water Pump		Door Locks	
Converter Ele. Sys.		Roof Vents	
Generator		Fire Extinguisher	
Refregererator		First Aid Kit	
Stove		Power Steps	
Microwave		Awnings	
Furnace		Slide Seals	
Coach Battery		Exterior Storage	
Water Heater		Smoke Detector	
Shower & Sinks		CO Detector	
Toilet		Upholstery	
Storage Cabinets		Roof Membrane	

Miles _____

Generator Engine Oil Type _____

Notes _____

RV Maintenance Log
CHASSIS

Date _____

Year _____ Make _____ Model _____ Serial # _____

Check	Condition	Check	Condition
Tire Pressure		Battery/Alternator	
Tire Wear/Age		Vehicle Lights	
Wheel Rims		Windshield Wipers	
Wheel Bearing/Seal		Tow Hitch	
Brake System		Switches	
Engine Oil		Mirrors	
Transmission		Differential	
Filters		Wiring	
Heating System		Belts and Hoses	
Cooling System		Power Steering	
Suspension/Shocks		Fuel Filter	
Water Pump		Chassis Lube	
Frame/Fastners		Cruise Control	
Air Conditioner		Horn	
Exhaust System		Airbags	
Gas Tank & Cap		Seatbelts	

Miles _____   Engine Oil Type _____

Notes _____

RV Maintenance Log

COACH BODY

Date _____

Year _____ Make _____ Model _____ Serial # _____

Check	Condition	Check	Condition
Dump Valve		Interior Lights	
Grey Water Tank		Air Conditioner	
Black Water Tank		Window Seals	
Fresh Water Tank		Window Locks	
Water Pump		Door Locks	
Converter Ele. Sys.		Roof Vents	
Generator		Fire Extinguisher	
Refrigererator		First Aid Kit	
Stove		Power Steps	
Microwave		Awnings	
Furnace		Slide Seals	
Coach Battery		Exterior Storage	
Water Heater		Smoke Detector	
Shower & Sinks		CO Detector	
Toilet		Upholstery	
Storage Cabinets		Roof Membrane	

Miles _____   Generator Engine Oil Type _____

Notes _____

RV Maintenance Log
CHASSIS

Date _____

Year _____ Make _____ Model _____ Serial # _____

Check	Condition	Check	Condition
Tire Pressure		Battery/Alternator	
Tire Wear/Age		Vehicle Lights	
Wheel Rims		Windshield Wipers	
Wheel Bearing/Seal		Tow Hitch	
Brake System		Switches	
Engine Oil		Mirrors	
Transmission		Differential	
Filters		Wiring	
Heating System		Belts and Hoses	
Cooling System		Power Steering	
Suspension/Shocks		Fuel Filter	
Water Pump		Chassis Lube	
Frame/Fastners		Cruise Control	
Air Conditioner		Horn	
Exhaust System		Airbags	
Gas Tank & Cap		Seatbelts	

Miles _____

Engine Oil Type _____

Notes _____

RV Maintenance Log

COACH BODY

Date _____

Year _____ Make _____ Model _____ Serial # _____

Check	Condition	Check	Condition
Dump Valve		Interior Lights	
Grey Water Tank		Air Conditioner	
Black Water Tank		Window Seals	
Fresh Water Tank		Window Locks	
Water Pump		Door Locks	
Converter Ele. Sys.		Roof Vents	
Generator		Fire Extinguisher	
Refrigererator		First Aid Kit	
Stove		Power Steps	
Microwave		Awnings	
Furnace		Slide Seals	
Coach Battery		Exterior Storage	
Water Heater		Smoke Detector	
Shower & Sinks		CO Detector	
Toilet		Upholstery	
Storage Cabinets		Roof Membrane	

Miles _____   Generator Engine Oil Type _____

Notes _____

RV Maintenance Log

CHASSIS

Date _____

Year _____ Make _____ Model _____ Serial # _____

Check	Condition	Check	Condition
Tire Pressure		Battery/Alternator	
Tire Wear/Age		Vehicle Lights	
Wheel Rims		Windshield Wipers	
Wheel Bearing/Seal		Tow Hitch	
Brake System		Switches	
Engine Oil		Mirrors	
Transmission		Differential	
Filters		Wiring	
Heating System		Belts and Hoses	
Cooling System		Power Steering	
Suspension/Shocks		Fuel Filter	
Water Pump		Chassis Lube	
Frame/Fastners		Cruise Control	
Air Conditioner		Horn	
Exhaust System		Airbags	
Gas Tank & Cap		Seatbelts	

Miles _____   Engine Oil Type _____

Notes _____

RV Maintenance Log
COACH BODY

Date _____

Year _____ Make _____ Model _____ Serial # _____

Check	Condition	Check	Condition
Dump Valve		Interior Lights	
Grey Water Tank		Air Conditioner	
Black Water Tank		Window Seals	
Fresh Water Tank		Window Locks	
Water Pump		Door Locks	
Converter Ele. Sys.		Roof Vents	
Generator		Fire Extinguisher	
Refrigererator		First Aid Kit	
Stove		Power Steps	
Microwave		Awnings	
Furnace		Slide Seals	
Coach Battery		Exterior Storage	
Water Heater		Smoke Detector	
Shower & Sinks		CO Detector	
Toilet		Upholstery	
Storage Cabinets		Roof Membrane	

Miles _____   Generator Engine Oil Type _____

Notes _____

RV Maintenance Log
CHASSIS

Date _____

Year _____ Make _____ Model _____ Serial # _____

Check	Condition	Check	Condition
Tire Pressure		Battery/Alternator	
Tire Wear/Age		Vehicle Lights	
Wheel Rims		Windshield Wipers	
Wheel Bearing/Seal		Tow Hitch	
Brake System		Switches	
Engine Oil		Mirrors	
Transmission		Differential	
Filters		Wiring	
Heating System		Belts and Hoses	
Cooling System		Power Steering	
Suspension/Shocks		Fuel Filter	
Water Pump		Chassis Lube	
Frame/Fastners		Cruise Control	
Air Conditioner		Horn	
Exhaust System		Airbags	
Gas Tank & Cap		Seatbelts	

Miles _____   Engine Oil Type _____

Notes _____

RV Maintenance Log

COACH BODY

Date _____

Year _____ Make _____ Model _____ Serial # _____

Check	Condition	Check	Condition
Dump Valve		Interior Lights	
Grey Water Tank		Air Conditioner	
Black Water Tank		Window Seals	
Fresh Water Tank		Window Locks	
Water Pump		Door Locks	
Converter Ele. Sys.		Roof Vents	
Generator		Fire Extinguisher	
Refrigererator		First Aid Kit	
Stove		Power Steps	
Microwave		Awnings	
Furnace		Slide Seals	
Coach Battery		Exterior Storage	
Water Heater		Smoke Detector	
Shower & Sinks		CO Detector	
Toilet		Upholstery	
Storage Cabinets		Roof Membrane	

Miles _____   Generator Engine Oil Type _____

Notes _____

RV Maintenance Log
CHASSIS

Date _____

Year _____ Make _____ Model _____ Serial # _____

Check	Condition	Check	Condition
Tire Pressure		Battery/Alternator	
Tire Wear/Age		Vehicle Lights	
Wheel Rims		Windshield Wipers	
Wheel Bearing/Seal		Tow Hitch	
Brake System		Switches	
Engine Oil		Mirrors	
Transmission		Differential	
Filters		Wiring	
Heating System		Belts and Hoses	
Cooling System		Power Steering	
Suspension/Shocks		Fuel Filter	
Water Pump		Chassis Lube	
Frame/Fastners		Cruise Control	
Air Conditioner		Horn	
Exhaust System		Airbags	
Gas Tank & Cap		Seatbelts	

Miles _____

Engine Oil Type _____

Notes _____

RV Maintenance Log

COACH BODY

RECREATIONAL VEHICLE
★ MAINTENANCE ★
— LOG —

Date _____

Year _____ Make _____ Model _____ Serial # _____

Check	Condition	Check	Condition
Dump Valve		Interior Lights	
Grey Water Tank		Air Conditioner	
Black Water Tank		Window Seals	
Fresh Water Tank		Window Locks	
Water Pump		Door Locks	
Converter Ele. Sys.		Roof Vents	
Generator		Fire Extinguisher	
Refrigererator		First Aid Kit	
Stove		Power Steps	
Microwave		Awnings	
Furnace		Slide Seals	
Coach Battery		Exterior Storage	
Water Heater		Smoke Detector	
Shower & Sinks		CO Detector	
Toilet		Upholstery	
Storage Cabinets		Roof Membrane	

Miles _____   Generator Engine Oil Type _____

Notes _____

RV Maintenance Log

CHASSIS

Date _____

Year _____ Make _____ Model _____ Serial # _____

Check	Condition	Check	Condition
Tire Pressure		Battery/Alternator	
Tire Wear/Age		Vehicle Lights	
Wheel Rims		Windshield Wipers	
Wheel Bearing/Seal		Tow Hitch	
Brake System		Switches	
Engine Oil		Mirrors	
Transmission		Differential	
Filters		Wiring	
Heating System		Belts and Hoses	
Cooling System		Power Steering	
Suspension/Shocks		Fuel Filter	
Water Pump		Chassis Lube	
Frame/Fastners		Cruise Control	
Air Conditioner		Horn	
Exhaust System		Airbags	
Gas Tank & Cap		Seatbelts	

Miles _____

Engine Oil Type _____

Notes _____

RV Maintenance Log

COACH BODY

Date _____

Year _____ Make _____ Model _____ Serial # _____

Check	Condition	Check	Condition
Dump Valve		Interior Lights	
Grey Water Tank		Air Conditioner	
Black Water Tank		Window Seals	
Fresh Water Tank		Window Locks	
Water Pump		Door Locks	
Converter Ele. Sys.		Roof Vents	
Generator		Fire Extinguisher	
Refrigererator		First Aid Kit	
Stove		Power Steps	
Microwave		Awnings	
Furnace		Slide Seals	
Coach Battery		Exterior Storage	
Water Heater		Smoke Detector	
Shower & Sinks		CO Detector	
Toilet		Upholstery	
Storage Cabinets		Roof Membrane	

Miles _____   Generator Engine Oil Type _____

Notes _____

RV Maintenance Log

CHASSIS

Date _____

Year _____ Make _____ Model _____ Serial # _____

Check	Condition	Check	Condition
Tire Pressure		Battery/Alternator	
Tire Wear/Age		Vehicle Lights	
Wheel Rims		Windshield Wipers	
Wheel Bearing/Seal		Tow Hitch	
Brake System		Switches	
Engine Oil		Mirrors	
Transmission		Differential	
Filters		Wiring	
Heating System		Belts and Hoses	
Cooling System		Power Steering	
Suspension/Shocks		Fuel Filter	
Water Pump		Chassis Lube	
Frame/Fastners		Cruise Control	
Air Conditioner		Horn	
Exhaust System		Airbags	
Gas Tank & Cap		Seatbelts	

Miles _____   Engine Oil Type _____

Notes _____

RV Maintenance Log

COACH BODY

RECREATIONAL VEHICLE
★ MAINTENANCE ★
— LOG —

Date _____

Year _____ Make _____ Model _____ Serial # _____

Check	Condition	Check	Condition
Dump Valve		Interior Lights	
Grey Water Tank		Air Conditioner	
Black Water Tank		Window Seals	
Fresh Water Tank		Window Locks	
Water Pump		Door Locks	
Converter Ele. Sys.		Roof Vents	
Generator		Fire Extinguisher	
Refrigererator		First Aid Kit	
Stove		Power Steps	
Microwave		Awnings	
Furnace		Slide Seals	
Coach Battery		Exterior Storage	
Water Heater		Smoke Detector	
Shower & Sinks		CO Detector	
Toilet		Upholstery	
Storage Cabinets		Roof Membrane	

Miles _____   Generator Engine Oil Type _____

Notes _____

RV Maintenance Log

CHASSIS

Date _____

Year _____ Make _____ Model _____ Serial # _____

Check	Condition	Check	Condition
Tire Pressure		Battery/Alternator	
Tire Wear/Age		Vehicle Lights	
Wheel Rims		Windshield Wipers	
Wheel Bearing/Seal		Tow Hitch	
Brake System		Switches	
Engine Oil		Mirrors	
Transmission		Differential	
Filters		Wiring	
Heating System		Belts and Hoses	
Cooling System		Power Steering	
Suspension/Shocks		Fuel Filter	
Water Pump		Chassis Lube	
Frame/Fastners		Cruise Control	
Air Conditioner		Horn	
Exhaust System		Airbags	
Gas Tank & Cap		Seatbelts	

Miles _____

Engine Oil Type _____

Notes _____

RV Maintenance Log

COACH BODY

RECREATIONAL VEHICLE
★ MAINTENANCE ★
— LOG —

Date _____

Year _____ Make _____ Model _____ Serial # _____

Check	Condition	Check	Condition
Dump Valve		Interior Lights	
Grey Water Tank		Air Conditioner	
Black Water Tank		Window Seals	
Fresh Water Tank		Window Locks	
Water Pump		Door Locks	
Converter Ele. Sys.		Roof Vents	
Generator		Fire Extinguisher	
Refrigererator		First Aid Kit	
Stove		Power Steps	
Microwave		Awnings	
Furnace		Slide Seals	
Coach Battery		Exterior Storage	
Water Heater		Smoke Detector	
Shower & Sinks		CO Detector	
Toilet		Upholstery	
Storage Cabinets		Roof Membrane	

Miles _____   Generator Engine Oil Type _____

Notes _____

RV Maintenance Log

CHASSIS

Date _____

Year _____ Make _____ Model _____ Serial # _____

Check	Condition	Check	Condition
Tire Pressure		Battery/Alternator	
Tire Wear/Age		Vehicle Lights	
Wheel Rims		Windshield Wipers	
Wheel Bearing/Seal		Tow Hitch	
Brake System		Switches	
Engine Oil		Mirrors	
Transmission		Differential	
Filters		Wiring	
Heating System		Belts and Hoses	
Cooling System		Power Steering	
Suspension/Shocks		Fuel Filter	
Water Pump		Chassis Lube	
Frame/Fastners		Cruise Control	
Air Conditioner		Horn	
Exhaust System		Airbags	
Gas Tank & Cap		Seatbelts	

Miles _____   Engine Oil Type _____

Notes _____

RV Maintenance Log
COACH BODY

Date _____

Year _____ Make _____ Model _____ Serial # _____

Check	Condition	Check	Condition
Dump Valve		Interior Lights	
Grey Water Tank		Air Conditioner	
Black Water Tank		Window Seals	
Fresh Water Tank		Window Locks	
Water Pump		Door Locks	
Converter Ele. Sys.		Roof Vents	
Generator		Fire Extinguisher	
Refrigererator		First Aid Kit	
Stove		Power Steps	
Microwave		Awnings	
Furnace		Slide Seals	
Coach Battery		Exterior Storage	
Water Heater		Smoke Detector	
Shower & Sinks		CO Detector	
Toilet		Upholstery	
Storage Cabinets		Roof Membrane	

Miles _____

Generator Engine Oil Type _____

Notes _____

RV Maintenance Log
CHASSIS

Date _____

Year _____ Make _____ Model _____ Serial # _____

Check	Condition	Check	Condition
Tire Pressure		Battery/Alternator	
Tire Wear/Age		Vehicle Lights	
Wheel Rims		Windshield Wipers	
Wheel Bearing/Seal		Tow Hitch	
Brake System		Switches	
Engine Oil		Mirrors	
Transmission		Differential	
Filters		Wiring	
Heating System		Belts and Hoses	
Cooling System		Power Steering	
Suspension/Shocks		Fuel Filter	
Water Pump		Chassis Lube	
Frame/Fastners		Cruise Control	
Air Conditioner		Horn	
Exhaust System		Airbags	
Gas Tank & Cap		Seatbelts	

Miles _____   Engine Oil Type _____

Notes _____

RV Maintenance Log

COACH BODY

Date _____

Year _____ Make _____ Model _____ Serial # _____

Check	Condition	Check	Condition
Dump Valve		Interior Lights	
Grey Water Tank		Air Conditioner	
Black Water Tank		Window Seals	
Fresh Water Tank		Window Locks	
Water Pump		Door Locks	
Converter Ele. Sys.		Roof Vents	
Generator		Fire Extinguisher	
Refrigererator		First Aid Kit	
Stove		Power Steps	
Microwave		Awnings	
Furnace		Slide Seals	
Coach Battery		Exterior Storage	
Water Heater		Smoke Detector	
Shower & Sinks		CO Detector	
Toilet		Upholstery	
Storage Cabinets		Roof Membrane	

Miles _____   Generator Engine Oil Type _____

Notes _____

RV Maintenance Log
CHASSIS

Date _____

Year _____ Make _____ Model _____ Serial # _____

Check	Condition	Check	Condition
Tire Pressure		Battery/Alternator	
Tire Wear/Age		Vehicle Lights	
Wheel Rims		Windshield Wipers	
Wheel Bearing/Seal		Tow Hitch	
Brake System		Switches	
Engine Oil		Mirrors	
Transmission		Differential	
Filters		Wiring	
Heating System		Belts and Hoses	
Cooling System		Power Steering	
Suspension/Shocks		Fuel Filter	
Water Pump		Chassis Lube	
Frame/Fastners		Cruise Control	
Air Conditioner		Horn	
Exhaust System		Airbags	
Gas Tank & Cap		Seatbelts	

Miles _____   Engine Oil Type _____

Notes _____

RV Maintenance Log

COACH BODY

Date _____

Year _____ Make _____ Model _____ Serial # _____

Check	Condition	Check	Condition
Dump Valve		Interior Lights	
Grey Water Tank		Air Conditioner	
Black Water Tank		Window Seals	
Fresh Water Tank		Window Locks	
Water Pump		Door Locks	
Converter Ele. Sys.		Roof Vents	
Generator		Fire Extinguisher	
Refrigererator		First Aid Kit	
Stove		Power Steps	
Microwave		Awnings	
Furnace		Slide Seals	
Coach Battery		Exterior Storage	
Water Heater		Smoke Detector	
Shower & Sinks		CO Detector	
Toilet		Upholstery	
Storage Cabinets		Roof Membrane	

Miles _____

Generator Engine Oil Type _____

Notes _____

RV Maintenance Log

CHASSIS

Date _____

Year _____ Make _____ Model _____ Serial # _____

Check	Condition	Check	Condition
Tire Pressure		Battery/Alternator	
Tire Wear/Age		Vehicle Lights	
Wheel Rims		Windshield Wipers	
Wheel Bearing/Seal		Tow Hitch	
Brake System		Switches	
Engine Oil		Mirrors	
Transmission		Differential	
Filters		Wiring	
Heating System		Belts and Hoses	
Cooling System		Power Steering	
Suspension/Shocks		Fuel Filter	
Water Pump		Chassis Lube	
Frame/Fastners		Cruise Control	
Air Conditioner		Horn	
Exhaust System		Airbags	
Gas Tank & Cap		Seatbelts	

Miles _____   Engine Oil Type _____

Notes _____

RV Maintenance Log

COACH BODY

Date _____

Year _____ Make _____ Model _____ Serial # _____

Check	Condition	Check	Condition
Dump Valve		Interior Lights	
Grey Water Tank		Air Conditioner	
Black Water Tank		Window Seals	
Fresh Water Tank		Window Locks	
Water Pump		Door Locks	
Converter Ele. Sys.		Roof Vents	
Generator		Fire Extinguisher	
Refrigererator		First Aid Kit	
Stove		Power Steps	
Microwave		Awnings	
Furnace		Slide Seals	
Coach Battery		Exterior Storage	
Water Heater		Smoke Detector	
Shower & Sinks		CO Detector	
Toilet		Upholstery	
Storage Cabinets		Roof Membrane	

Miles _____   Generator Engine Oil Type _____

Notes _____

RV Maintenance Log

CHASSIS

Date _____

Year _____ Make _____ Model _____ Serial # _____

Check	Condition	Check	Condition
Tire Pressure		Battery/Alternator	
Tire Wear/Age		Vehicle Lights	
Wheel Rims		Windshield Wipers	
Wheel Bearing/Seal		Tow Hitch	
Brake System		Switches	
Engine Oil		Mirrors	
Transmission		Differential	
Filters		Wiring	
Heating System		Belts and Hoses	
Cooling System		Power Steering	
Suspension/Shocks		Fuel Filter	
Water Pump		Chassis Lube	
Frame/Fastners		Cruise Control	
Air Conditioner		Horn	
Exhaust System		Airbags	
Gas Tank & Cap		Seatbelts	

Miles _____   Engine Oil Type _____

Notes _____

RV Maintenance Log
COACH BODY

RECREATIONAL VEHICLE
★ MAINTENANCE ★
— LOG —

Date _____

Year _____ Make _____ Model _____ Serial # _____

Check	Condition	Check	Condition
Dump Valve		Interior Lights	
Grey Water Tank		Air Conditioner	
Black Water Tank		Window Seals	
Fresh Water Tank		Window Locks	
Water Pump		Door Locks	
Converter Ele. Sys.		Roof Vents	
Generator		Fire Extinguisher	
Refrigererator		First Aid Kit	
Stove		Power Steps	
Microwave		Awnings	
Furnace		Slide Seals	
Coach Battery		Exterior Storage	
Water Heater		Smoke Detector	
Shower & Sinks		CO Detector	
Toilet		Upholstery	
Storage Cabinets		Roof Membrane	

Miles _____   Generator Engine Oil Type _____

Notes _____

RV Maintenance Log
CHASSIS

Date _____

Year _____   Make _____   Model _____   Serial # _____

Check	Condition	Check	Condition
Tire Pressure		Battery/Alternator	
Tire Wear/Age		Vehicle Lights	
Wheel Rims		Windshield Wipers	
Wheel Bearing/Seal		Tow Hitch	
Brake System		Switches	
Engine Oil		Mirrors	
Transmission		Differential	
Filters		Wiring	
Heating System		Belts and Hoses	
Cooling System		Power Steering	
Suspension/Shocks		Fuel Filter	
Water Pump		Chassis Lube	
Frame/Fastners		Cruise Control	
Air Conditioner		Horn	
Exhaust System		Airbags	
Gas Tank & Cap		Seatbelts	

Miles _____   Engine Oil Type _____

Notes _____

RV Maintenance Log

COACH BODY

Date _____

Year _____ Make _____ Model _____ Serial # _____

Check	Condition	Check	Condition
Dump Valve		Interior Lights	
Grey Water Tank		Air Conditioner	
Black Water Tank		Window Seals	
Fresh Water Tank		Window Locks	
Water Pump		Door Locks	
Converter Ele. Sys.		Roof Vents	
Generator		Fire Extinguisher	
Refrigererator		First Aid Kit	
Stove		Power Steps	
Microwave		Awnings	
Furnace		Slide Seals	
Coach Battery		Exterior Storage	
Water Heater		Smoke Detector	
Shower & Sinks		CO Detector	
Toilet		Upholstery	
Storage Cabinets		Roof Membrane	

Miles _____

Generator Engine Oil Type _____

Notes _____

RV Maintenance Log
CHASSIS

Date _____

Year _____ Make _____ Model _____ Serial # _____

Check	Condition	Check	Condition
Tire Pressure		Battery/Alternator	
Tire Wear/Age		Vehicle Lights	
Wheel Rims		Windshield Wipers	
Wheel Bearing/Seal		Tow Hitch	
Brake System		Switches	
Engine Oil		Mirrors	
Transmission		Differential	
Filters		Wiring	
Heating System		Belts and Hoses	
Cooling System		Power Steering	
Suspension/Shocks		Fuel Filter	
Water Pump		Chassis Lube	
Frame/Fastners		Cruise Control	
Air Conditioner		Horn	
Exhaust System		Airbags	
Gas Tank & Cap		Seatbelts	

Miles _____   Engine Oil Type _____

Notes _____

RV Maintenance Log
COACH BODY

Date _____

Year _____ Make _____ Model _____ Serial # _____

Check	Condition	Check	Condition
Dump Valve		Interior Lights	
Grey Water Tank		Air Conditioner	
Black Water Tank		Window Seals	
Fresh Water Tank		Window Locks	
Water Pump		Door Locks	
Converter Ele. Sys.		Roof Vents	
Generator		Fire Extinguisher	
Refrigererator		First Aid Kit	
Stove		Power Steps	
Microwave		Awnings	
Furnace		Slide Seals	
Coach Battery		Exterior Storage	
Water Heater		Smoke Detector	
Shower & Sinks		CO Detector	
Toilet		Upholstery	
Storage Cabinets		Roof Membrane	

Miles _____   Generator Engine Oil Type _____

Notes _____

RV Maintenance Log

CHASSIS

Date _____

Year _____ Make _____ Model _____ Serial # _____

Check	Condition	Check	Condition
Tire Pressure		Battery/Alternator	
Tire Wear/Age		Vehicle Lights	
Wheel Rims		Windshield Wipers	
Wheel Bearing/Seal		Tow Hitch	
Brake System		Switches	
Engine Oil		Mirrors	
Transmission		Differential	
Filters		Wiring	
Heating System		Belts and Hoses	
Cooling System		Power Steering	
Suspension/Shocks		Fuel Filter	
Water Pump		Chassis Lube	
Frame/Fastners		Cruise Control	
Air Conditioner		Horn	
Exhaust System		Airbags	
Gas Tank & Cap		Seatbelts	

Miles _____   Engine Oil Type _____

Notes _____

RV Maintenance Log

COACH BODY

Date _____

Year _____ Make _____ Model _____ Serial # _____

Check	Condition	Check	Condition
Dump Valve		Interior Lights	
Grey Water Tank		Air Conditioner	
Black Water Tank		Window Seals	
Fresh Water Tank		Window Locks	
Water Pump		Door Locks	
Converter Ele. Sys.		Roof Vents	
Generator		Fire Extinguisher	
Refrigererator		First Aid Kit	
Stove		Power Steps	
Microwave		Awnings	
Furnace		Slide Seals	
Coach Battery		Exterior Storage	
Water Heater		Smoke Detector	
Shower & Sinks		CO Detector	
Toilet		Upholstery	
Storage Cabinets		Roof Membrane	

Miles _____   Generator Engine Oil Type _____

Notes _____

RV Maintenance Log

CHASSIS

Date _____

Year _____ Make _____ Model _____ Serial # _____

Check	Condition	Check	Condition
Tire Pressure		Battery/Alternator	
Tire Wear/Age		Vehicle Lights	
Wheel Rims		Windshield Wipers	
Wheel Bearing/Seal		Tow Hitch	
Brake System		Switches	
Engine Oil		Mirrors	
Transmission		Differential	
Filters		Wiring	
Heating System		Belts and Hoses	
Cooling System		Power Steering	
Suspension/Shocks		Fuel Filter	
Water Pump		Chassis Lube	
Frame/Fastners		Cruise Control	
Air Conditioner		Horn	
Exhaust System		Airbags	
Gas Tank & Cap		Seatbelts	

Miles _____   Engine Oil Type _____

Notes _____

RV Maintenance Log
COACH BODY

Date _____

Year _____ Make _____ Model _____ Serial # _____

Check	Condition	Check	Condition
Dump Valve		Interior Lights	
Grey Water Tank		Air Conditioner	
Black Water Tank		Window Seals	
Fresh Water Tank		Window Locks	
Water Pump		Door Locks	
Converter Ele. Sys.		Roof Vents	
Generator		Fire Extinguisher	
Refrigererator		First Aid Kit	
Stove		Power Steps	
Microwave		Awnings	
Furnace		Slide Seals	
Coach Battery		Exterior Storage	
Water Heater		Smoke Detector	
Shower & Sinks		CO Detector	
Toilet		Upholstery	
Storage Cabinets		Roof Membrane	

Miles _____   Generator Engine Oil Type _____

Notes _____

RV Maintenance Log

CHASSIS

Date _____

Year _____ Make _____ Model _____ Serial # _____

Check	Condition	Check	Condition
Tire Pressure		Battery/Alternator	
Tire Wear/Age		Vehicle Lights	
Wheel Rims		Windshield Wipers	
Wheel Bearing/Seal		Tow Hitch	
Brake System		Switches	
Engine Oil		Mirrors	
Transmission		Differential	
Filters		Wiring	
Heating System		Belts and Hoses	
Cooling System		Power Steering	
Suspension/Shocks		Fuel Filter	
Water Pump		Chassis Lube	
Frame/Fastners		Cruise Control	
Air Conditioner		Horn	
Exhaust System		Airbags	
Gas Tank & Cap		Seatbelts	

Miles _____   Engine Oil Type _____

Notes _____

RV Maintenance Log

COACH BODY

Date _____

Year _____ Make _____ Model _____ Serial # _____

Check	Condition	Check	Condition
Dump Valve		Interior Lights	
Grey Water Tank		Air Conditioner	
Black Water Tank		Window Seals	
Fresh Water Tank		Window Locks	
Water Pump		Door Locks	
Converter Ele. Sys.		Roof Vents	
Generator		Fire Extinguisher	
Refrigererator		First Aid Kit	
Stove		Power Steps	
Microwave		Awnings	
Furnace		Slide Seals	
Coach Battery		Exterior Storage	
Water Heater		Smoke Detector	
Shower & Sinks		CO Detector	
Toilet		Upholstery	
Storage Cabinets		Roof Membrane	

Miles _____   Generator Engine Oil Type _____

Notes _____

RV Maintenance Log
CHASSIS

Date _____

Year _____ Make _____ Model _____ Serial # _____

Check	Condition	Check	Condition
Tire Pressure		Battery/Alternator	
Tire Wear/Age		Vehicle Lights	
Wheel Rims		Windshield Wipers	
Wheel Bearing/Seal		Tow Hitch	
Brake System		Switches	
Engine Oil		Mirrors	
Transmission		Differential	
Filters		Wiring	
Heating System		Belts and Hoses	
Cooling System		Power Steering	
Suspension/Shocks		Fuel Filter	
Water Pump		Chassis Lube	
Frame/Fastners		Cruise Control	
Air Conditioner		Horn	
Exhaust System		Airbags	
Gas Tank & Cap		Seatbelts	

Miles _____

Engine Oil Type _____

Notes _____

RV Maintenance Log

COACH BODY

RECREATIONAL VEHICLE
★ MAINTENANCE ★
— LOG —

Date _____

Year _____ Make _____ Model _____ Serial # _____

Check	Condition	Check	Condition
Dump Valve		Interior Lights	
Grey Water Tank		Air Conditioner	
Black Water Tank		Window Seals	
Fresh Water Tank		Window Locks	
Water Pump		Door Locks	
Converter Ele. Sys.		Roof Vents	
Generator		Fire Extinguisher	
Refrigererator		First Aid Kit	
Stove		Power Steps	
Microwave		Awnings	
Furnace		Slide Seals	
Coach Battery		Exterior Storage	
Water Heater		Smoke Detector	
Shower & Sinks		CO Detector	
Toilet		Upholstery	
Storage Cabinets		Roof Membrane	

Miles _____   Generator Engine Oil Type _____

Notes _____

RV Maintenance Log

CHASSIS

Date _____

Year _____ Make _____ Model _____ Serial # _____

Check	Condition	Check	Condition
Tire Pressure		Battery/Alternator	
Tire Wear/Age		Vehicle Lights	
Wheel Rims		Windshield Wipers	
Wheel Bearing/Seal		Tow Hitch	
Brake System		Switches	
Engine Oil		Mirrors	
Transmission		Differential	
Filters		Wiring	
Heating System		Belts and Hoses	
Cooling System		Power Steering	
Suspension/Shocks		Fuel Filter	
Water Pump		Chassis Lube	
Frame/Fastners		Cruise Control	
Air Conditioner		Horn	
Exhaust System		Airbags	
Gas Tank & Cap		Seatbelts	

Miles _____   Engine Oil Type _____

Notes _____

RV Maintenance Log
COACH BODY

Date _____

Year _____ Make _____ Model _____ Serial # _____

Check	Condition	Check	Condition
Dump Valve		Interior Lights	
Grey Water Tank		Air Conditioner	
Black Water Tank		Window Seals	
Fresh Water Tank		Window Locks	
Water Pump		Door Locks	
Converter Ele. Sys.		Roof Vents	
Generator		Fire Extinguisher	
Refrigererator		First Aid Kit	
Stove		Power Steps	
Microwave		Awnings	
Furnace		Slide Seals	
Coach Battery		Exterior Storage	
Water Heater		Smoke Detector	
Shower & Sinks		CO Detector	
Toilet		Upholstery	
Storage Cabinets		Roof Membrane	

Miles _____   Generator Engine Oil Type _____

Notes _____

RV Maintenance Log

CHASSIS

Date _____

Year _____ Make _____ Model _____ Serial # _____

Check	Condition	Check	Condition
Tire Pressure		Battery/Alternator	
Tire Wear/Age		Vehicle Lights	
Wheel Rims		Windshield Wipers	
Wheel Bearing/Seal		Tow Hitch	
Brake System		Switches	
Engine Oil		Mirrors	
Transmission		Differential	
Filters		Wiring	
Heating System		Belts and Hoses	
Cooling System		Power Steering	
Suspension/Shocks		Fuel Filter	
Water Pump		Chassis Lube	
Frame/Fastners		Cruise Control	
Air Conditioner		Horn	
Exhaust System		Airbags	
Gas Tank & Cap		Seatbelts	

Miles _____   Engine Oil Type _____

Notes _____

RV Maintenance Log

COACH BODY

RECREATIONAL VEHICLE
★ MAINTENANCE ★
— LOG —

Date _____

Year _____ Make _____ Model _____ Serial # _____

Check	Condition	Check	Condition
Dump Valve		Interior Lights	
Grey Water Tank		Air Conditioner	
Black Water Tank		Window Seals	
Fresh Water Tank		Window Locks	
Water Pump		Door Locks	
Converter Ele. Sys.		Roof Vents	
Generator		Fire Extinguisher	
Refrigererator		First Aid Kit	
Stove		Power Steps	
Microwave		Awnings	
Furnace		Slide Seals	
Coach Battery		Exterior Storage	
Water Heater		Smoke Detector	
Shower & Sinks		CO Detector	
Toilet		Upholstery	
Storage Cabinets		Roof Membrane	

Miles _____

Generator Engine Oil Type _____

Notes _____

RV Maintenance Log

CHASSIS

RECREATIONAL VEHICLE
★ MAINTENANCE ★
— LOG —

Date _____

Year _____ Make _____ Model _____ Serial # _____

Check	Condition	Check	Condition
Tire Pressure		Battery/Alternator	
Tire Wear/Age		Vehicle Lights	
Wheel Rims		Windshield Wipers	
Wheel Bearing/Seal		Tow Hitch	
Brake System		Switches	
Engine Oil		Mirrors	
Transmission		Differential	
Filters		Wiring	
Heating System		Belts and Hoses	
Cooling System		Power Steering	
Suspension/Shocks		Fuel Filter	
Water Pump		Chassis Lube	
Frame/Fastners		Cruise Control	
Air Conditioner		Horn	
Exhaust System		Airbags	
Gas Tank & Cap		Seatbelts	

Miles _____

Engine Oil Type _____

Notes _____

RV Maintenance Log

COACH BODY

Date _____

Year _____ Make _____ Model _____ Serial # _____

Check	Condition	Check	Condition
Dump Valve		Interior Lights	
Grey Water Tank		Air Conditioner	
Black Water Tank		Window Seals	
Fresh Water Tank		Window Locks	
Water Pump		Door Locks	
Converter Ele. Sys.		Roof Vents	
Generator		Fire Extinguisher	
Refrigererator		First Aid Kit	
Stove		Power Steps	
Microwave		Awnings	
Furnace		Slide Seals	
Coach Battery		Exterior Storage	
Water Heater		Smoke Detector	
Shower & Sinks		CO Detector	
Toilet		Upholstery	
Storage Cabinets		Roof Membrane	

Miles _____   Generator Engine Oil Type _____

Notes _____

RV Maintenance Log

CHASSIS

Date _____

Year _____ Make _____ Model _____ Serial # _____

Check	Condition	Check	Condition
Tire Pressure		Battery/Alternator	
Tire Wear/Age		Vehicle Lights	
Wheel Rims		Windshield Wipers	
Wheel Bearing/Seal		Tow Hitch	
Brake System		Switches	
Engine Oil		Mirrors	
Transmission		Differential	
Filters		Wiring	
Heating System		Belts and Hoses	
Cooling System		Power Steering	
Suspension/Shocks		Fuel Filter	
Water Pump		Chassis Lube	
Frame/Fastners		Cruise Control	
Air Conditioner		Horn	
Exhaust System		Airbags	
Gas Tank & Cap		Seatbelts	

Miles _____   Engine Oil Type _____

Notes _____

RV Maintenance Log
COACH BODY

RECREATIONAL VEHICLE
★ MAINTENANCE ★
— LOG —

Date _____

Year _____ Make _____ Model _____ Serial # _____

Check	Condition	Check	Condition
Dump Valve		Interior Lights	
Grey Water Tank		Air Conditioner	
Black Water Tank		Window Seals	
Fresh Water Tank		Window Locks	
Water Pump		Door Locks	
Converter Ele. Sys.		Roof Vents	
Generator		Fire Extinguisher	
Refrigererator		First Aid Kit	
Stove		Power Steps	
Microwave		Awnings	
Furnace		Slide Seals	
Coach Battery		Exterior Storage	
Water Heater		Smoke Detector	
Shower & Sinks		CO Detector	
Toilet		Upholstery	
Storage Cabinets		Roof Membrane	

Miles _____ Generator Engine Oil Type _____

Notes _____

RV Maintenance Log

CHASSIS

Date _____

Year _____ Make _____ Model _____ Serial # _____

Check	Condition	Check	Condition
Tire Pressure		Battery/Alternator	
Tire Wear/Age		Vehicle Lights	
Wheel Rims		Windshield Wipers	
Wheel Bearing/Seal		Tow Hitch	
Brake System		Switches	
Engine Oil		Mirrors	
Transmission		Differential	
Filters		Wiring	
Heating System		Belts and Hoses	
Cooling System		Power Steering	
Suspension/Shocks		Fuel Filter	
Water Pump		Chassis Lube	
Frame/Fastners		Cruise Control	
Air Conditioner		Horn	
Exhaust System		Airbags	
Gas Tank & Cap		Seatbelts	

Miles _____   Engine Oil Type _____

Notes

RV Maintenance Log
COACH BODY

Date _____

Year _____ Make _____ Model _____ Serial # _____

Check	Condition	Check	Condition
Dump Valve		Interior Lights	
Grey Water Tank		Air Conditioner	
Black Water Tank		Window Seals	
Fresh Water Tank		Window Locks	
Water Pump		Door Locks	
Converter Ele. Sys.		Roof Vents	
Generator		Fire Extinguisher	
Refrigererator		First Aid Kit	
Stove		Power Steps	
Microwave		Awnings	
Furnace		Slide Seals	
Coach Battery		Exterior Storage	
Water Heater		Smoke Detector	
Shower & Sinks		CO Detector	
Toilet		Upholstery	
Storage Cabinets		Roof Membrane	

Miles _____   Generator Engine Oil Type _____

Notes _____

RV Maintenance Log

CHASSIS

Date _____

Year _____ Make _____ Model _____ Serial # _____

Check	Condition	Check	Condition
Tire Pressure		Battery/Alternator	
Tire Wear/Age		Vehicle Lights	
Wheel Rims		Windshield Wipers	
Wheel Bearing/Seal		Tow Hitch	
Brake System		Switches	
Engine Oil		Mirrors	
Transmission		Differential	
Filters		Wiring	
Heating System		Belts and Hoses	
Cooling System		Power Steering	
Suspension/Shocks		Fuel Filter	
Water Pump		Chassis Lube	
Frame/Fastners		Cruise Control	
Air Conditioner		Horn	
Exhaust System		Airbags	
Gas Tank & Cap		Seatbelts	

Miles _____

Engine Oil Type _____

Notes

RV Maintenance Log

COACH BODY

Date _____

Year _____ Make _____ Model _____ Serial # _____

Check	Condition	Check	Condition
Dump Valve		Interior Lights	
Grey Water Tank		Air Conditioner	
Black Water Tank		Window Seals	
Fresh Water Tank		Window Locks	
Water Pump		Door Locks	
Converter Ele. Sys.		Roof Vents	
Generator		Fire Extinguisher	
Refrigererator		First Aid Kit	
Stove		Power Steps	
Microwave		Awnings	
Furnace		Slide Seals	
Coach Battery		Exterior Storage	
Water Heater		Smoke Detector	
Shower & Sinks		CO Detector	
Toilet		Upholstery	
Storage Cabinets		Roof Membrane	

Miles _____   Generator Engine Oil Type _____

Notes _____

RV Maintenance Log

CHASSIS

Date _____

Year _____ Make _____ Model _____ Serial # _____

Check	Condition	Check	Condition
Tire Pressure		Battery/Alternator	
Tire Wear/Age		Vehicle Lights	
Wheel Rims		Windshield Wipers	
Wheel Bearing/Seal		Tow Hitch	
Brake System		Switches	
Engine Oil		Mirrors	
Transmission		Differential	
Filters		Wiring	
Heating System		Belts and Hoses	
Cooling System		Power Steering	
Suspension/Shocks		Fuel Filter	
Water Pump		Chassis Lube	
Frame/Fastners		Cruise Control	
Air Conditioner		Horn	
Exhaust System		Airbags	
Gas Tank & Cap		Seatbelts	

Miles _____   Engine Oil Type _____

Notes _____

RV Maintenance Log
COACH BODY

Date _____

Year _____ Make _____ Model _____ Serial # _____

Check	Condition	Check	Condition
Dump Valve		Interior Lights	
Grey Water Tank		Air Conditioner	
Black Water Tank		Window Seals	
Fresh Water Tank		Window Locks	
Water Pump		Door Locks	
Converter Ele. Sys.		Roof Vents	
Generator		Fire Extinguisher	
Refrigererator		First Aid Kit	
Stove		Power Steps	
Microwave		Awnings	
Furnace		Slide Seals	
Coach Battery		Exterior Storage	
Water Heater		Smoke Detector	
Shower & Sinks		CO Detector	
Toilet		Upholstery	
Storage Cabinets		Roof Membrane	

Miles _____   Generator Engine Oil Type _____

Notes _____

RV Maintenance Log
CHASSIS

Date _____

Year _____ Make _____ Model _____ Serial # _____

Check	Condition	Check	Condition
Tire Pressure		Battery/Alternator	
Tire Wear/Age		Vehicle Lights	
Wheel Rims		Windshield Wipers	
Wheel Bearing/Seal		Tow Hitch	
Brake System		Switches	
Engine Oil		Mirrors	
Transmission		Differential	
Filters		Wiring	
Heating System		Belts and Hoses	
Cooling System		Power Steering	
Suspension/Shocks		Fuel Filter	
Water Pump		Chassis Lube	
Frame/Fastners		Cruise Control	
Air Conditioner		Horn	
Exhaust System		Airbags	
Gas Tank & Cap		Seatbelts	

Miles _____   Engine Oil Type _____

Notes _____

RV Maintenance Log
COACH BODY

Date _____

Year _____ Make _____ Model _____ Serial # _____

Check	Condition	Check	Condition
Dump Valve		Interior Lights	
Grey Water Tank		Air Conditioner	
Black Water Tank		Window Seals	
Fresh Water Tank		Window Locks	
Water Pump		Door Locks	
Converter Ele. Sys.		Roof Vents	
Generator		Fire Extinguisher	
Refrigererator		First Aid Kit	
Stove		Power Steps	
Microwave		Awnings	
Furnace		Slide Seals	
Coach Battery		Exterior Storage	
Water Heater		Smoke Detector	
Shower & Sinks		CO Detector	
Toilet		Upholstery	
Storage Cabinets		Roof Membrane	

Miles _____   Generator Engine Oil Type _____

Notes _____

RV Maintenance Log
CHASSIS

Date _____

Year _____ Make _____ Model _____ Serial # _____

Check	Condition	Check	Condition
Tire Pressure		Battery/Alternator	
Tire Wear/Age		Vehicle Lights	
Wheel Rims		Windshield Wipers	
Wheel Bearing/Seal		Tow Hitch	
Brake System		Switches	
Engine Oil		Mirrors	
Transmission		Differential	
Filters		Wiring	
Heating System		Belts and Hoses	
Cooling System		Power Steering	
Suspension/Shocks		Fuel Filter	
Water Pump		Chassis Lube	
Frame/Fastners		Cruise Control	
Air Conditioner		Horn	
Exhaust System		Airbags	
Gas Tank & Cap		Seatbelts	

Miles _____

Engine Oil Type _____

Notes

RV Maintenance Log

COACH BODY

Date _____

Year _____ Make _____ Model _____ Serial # _____

Check	Condition	Check	Condition
Dump Valve		Interior Lights	
Grey Water Tank		Air Conditioner	
Black Water Tank		Window Seals	
Fresh Water Tank		Window Locks	
Water Pump		Door Locks	
Converter Ele. Sys.		Roof Vents	
Generator		Fire Extinguisher	
Refrigererator		First Aid Kit	
Stove		Power Steps	
Microwave		Awnings	
Furnace		Slide Seals	
Coach Battery		Exterior Storage	
Water Heater		Smoke Detector	
Shower & Sinks		CO Detector	
Toilet		Upholstery	
Storage Cabinets		Roof Membrane	

Miles _____ Generator Engine Oil Type _____

Notes _____

RV Maintenance Log

CHASSIS

Date _____

Year _____ Make _____ Model _____ Serial # _____

Check	Condition	Check	Condition
Tire Pressure		Battery/Alternator	
Tire Wear/Age		Vehicle Lights	
Wheel Rims		Windshield Wipers	
Wheel Bearing/Seal		Tow Hitch	
Brake System		Switches	
Engine Oil		Mirrors	
Transmission		Differential	
Filters		Wiring	
Heating System		Belts and Hoses	
Cooling System		Power Steering	
Suspension/Shocks		Fuel Filter	
Water Pump		Chassis Lube	
Frame/Fastners		Cruise Control	
Air Conditioner		Horn	
Exhaust System		Airbags	
Gas Tank & Cap		Seatbelts	

Miles _____   Engine Oil Type _____

Notes _____

RV Maintenance Log
COACH BODY

Date _____

Year _____ Make _____ Model _____ Serial # _____

Check	Condition	Check	Condition
Dump Valve		Interior Lights	
Grey Water Tank		Air Conditioner	
Black Water Tank		Window Seals	
Fresh Water Tank		Window Locks	
Water Pump		Door Locks	
Converter Ele. Sys.		Roof Vents	
Generator		Fire Extinguisher	
Refrigererator		First Aid Kit	
Stove		Power Steps	
Microwave		Awnings	
Furnace		Slide Seals	
Coach Battery		Exterior Storage	
Water Heater		Smoke Detector	
Shower & Sinks		CO Detector	
Toilet		Upholstery	
Storage Cabinets		Roof Membrane	

Miles _____   Generator Engine Oil Type _____

Notes _____

RV Maintenance Log

CHASSIS

Date _____

Year _____ Make _____ Model _____ Serial # _____

Check	Condition	Check	Condition
Tire Pressure		Battery/Alternator	
Tire Wear/Age		Vehicle Lights	
Wheel Rims		Windshield Wipers	
Wheel Bearing/Seal		Tow Hitch	
Brake System		Switches	
Engine Oil		Mirrors	
Transmission		Differential	
Filters		Wiring	
Heating System		Belts and Hoses	
Cooling System		Power Steering	
Suspension/Shocks		Fuel Filter	
Water Pump		Chassis Lube	
Frame/Fastners		Cruise Control	
Air Conditioner		Horn	
Exhaust System		Airbags	
Gas Tank & Cap		Seatbelts	

Miles _____

Engine Oil Type _____

Notes _____

RV Maintenance Log
COACH BODY

Date _____

Year _____ Make _____ Model _____ Serial # _____

Check	Condition	Check	Condition
Dump Valve		Interior Lights	
Grey Water Tank		Air Conditioner	
Black Water Tank		Window Seals	
Fresh Water Tank		Window Locks	
Water Pump		Door Locks	
Converter Ele. Sys.		Roof Vents	
Generator		Fire Extinguisher	
Refrigererator		First Aid Kit	
Stove		Power Steps	
Microwave		Awnings	
Furnace		Slide Seals	
Coach Battery		Exterior Storage	
Water Heater		Smoke Detector	
Shower & Sinks		CO Detector	
Toilet		Upholstery	
Storage Cabinets		Roof Membrane	

Miles _____   Generator Engine Oil Type _____

Notes _____

RV Maintenance Log

CHASSIS

Date _____

Year _____ Make _____ Model _____ Serial # _____

Check	Condition	Check	Condition
Tire Pressure		Battery/Alternator	
Tire Wear/Age		Vehicle Lights	
Wheel Rims		Windshield Wipers	
Wheel Bearing/Seal		Tow Hitch	
Brake System		Switches	
Engine Oil		Mirrors	
Transmission		Differential	
Filters		Wiring	
Heating System		Belts and Hoses	
Cooling System		Power Steering	
Suspension/Shocks		Fuel Filter	
Water Pump		Chassis Lube	
Frame/Fastners		Cruise Control	
Air Conditioner		Horn	
Exhaust System		Airbags	
Gas Tank & Cap		Seatbelts	

Miles _____   Engine Oil Type _____

Notes _____

RV Maintenance Log
COACH BODY

Date _____

Year _____ Make _____ Model _____ Serial # _____

Check	Condition	Check	Condition
Dump Valve		Interior Lights	
Grey Water Tank		Air Conditioner	
Black Water Tank		Window Seals	
Fresh Water Tank		Window Locks	
Water Pump		Door Locks	
Converter Ele. Sys.		Roof Vents	
Generator		Fire Extinguisher	
Refrigererator		First Aid Kit	
Stove		Power Steps	
Microwave		Awnings	
Furnace		Slide Seals	
Coach Battery		Exterior Storage	
Water Heater		Smoke Detector	
Shower & Sinks		CO Detector	
Toilet		Upholstery	
Storage Cabinets		Roof Membrane	

Miles _____ Generator Engine Oil Type _____

Notes _____

NOTES

NOTES

NOTES

NOTES

NOTES

NOTES

NOTES

NOTES

NOTES

Made in United States
Troutdale, OR
09/02/2023

12580640R00062